Life in the  New American Nation™

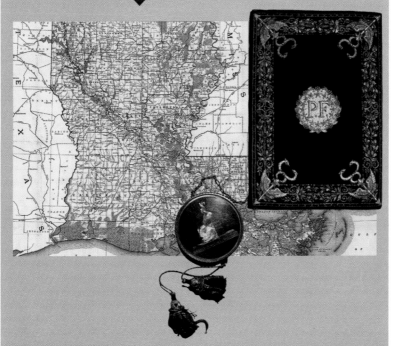

# The Louisiana Purchase

Expanding America's Boundaries

Magdalena Alagna

rosen central
**Primary Source**™

The Rosen Publishing Group, Inc., New York

Published in 2004 by The Rosen Publishing Group, Inc.
29 East 21st Street, New York, NY 10010

**Library of Congress Cataloging-in-Publication Data**

Alagna, Magdalena.
The Louisiana Purchase: expanding America's boundaries / by Magdalena Alagna. — 1st ed.
     p. cm. — (Life in the new American nation)
Summary: Explains the events surrounding the Louisiana Purchase, through which President Jefferson acquired enough land to make the United States one of the largest nations in the world. Includes bibliographical references (p.   ) and index.
ISBN 0-8239-4039-X (lib. bdg.)
ISBN 0-8239-4257-0 (pbk. bdg.)
6-pack ISBN 0-8239-4270-8
1. Louisiana Purchase—Juvenile literature. [1. Louisiana Purchase. 2. United States—Territorial expansion.] I. Title. II. Series.
E333.A43 2003
973.4'6—dc21

                                                                    2002154616


*Manufactured in the United States of America*

Cover (left): Copy of the Louisiana Purchase
Cover (right): View of New Orleans riverfront

Photo credits: cover, pp. 6, 16 (bottom), 19 (top), 23 courtesy of Library of Congress; pp. 1, 24 © National Archive and Records Administration; pp. 5, 12, 14 (left and right), 25, 27 © AP/World Wide Photos; p. 9 © Hulton/Archive/Getty Images; p. 10 © Gianni Dagli/Orti/Corbis; p. 16 (top) © Bettmann/Corbis; p. 19 (bottom) © Architect of the Capitol.

Designer: Nelson Sá; Editor: Eliza Berkowitz; Photo Researcher: Nelson Sá

# Contents

# Introduction

In 1803, Thomas Jefferson, president of the United States, bought land from France. The sale of this land ended the threat of having to go to war with France for control of the port of New Orleans. It also opened up the western part of North America to settlers. With the stroke of a pen, Jefferson inked a deal that made America one of the largest nations in the world. The Louisiana Purchase doubled the size of the United States. The land measured 828,000 square miles (2,144,520 square kilometers).

The land was known as the Louisiana Territory. It was located west of the Mississippi River to the Rocky Mountains. It stretched from the Gulf of Mexico to Canada. The buying of the land was called the Louisiana Purchase.

Spain and France had been fighting for control of the Louisiana Territory for many years. That's because

This portrait of Thomas Jefferson, the third president of the United States, was created by Thomas Scully in 1821. Jefferson signed the deal in which France sold the Louisiana Territory to the United States. This land was very valuable. It made the United States able to trade from the port of New Orleans. It also let the United States expand westward.

the territory was a valuable one to control. The land included the city and the port of New Orleans. The port was an important place for trade. Whoever owned the land could sail from the Gulf of Mexico to the Mississippi River. That was a key trade route. Also, the owner could use New Orleans as a point of deposit. A point of deposit is a place to store goods. Many ships kept goods in warehouses in the port of New Orleans until they were ready to be shipped somewhere else.

**THE CITY OF NEW ORLEANS,**
AND THE MISSISSIPPI RIVER. LAKE PONTCHARTRAIN IN DISTANCE.

NEW YORK, PUBLISHED BY CURRIER & IVES, 115 NASSAU ST.

This is a panoramic map of the city of New Orleans. The city was part of the Louisiana Territory and was fought over for many years. One of the reasons it was fought over was because it was right on the water, making it an ideal place for trading.

6

Owning the Louisiana Territory meant something special for America. For America to own this land meant that there would be no European power to stop the westward expansion. The westward expansion is the name given to the movement of settlers to the unsettled parts of western America in the 1800s. Also, the United States would gain respect in Europe. This is because the purchase would make the United States one of the largest nations in the world. Finally, the Louisiana Purchase tested the powers of the Constitution. America was a new country, and the Constitution was a new document. No one was sure how the laws in the Constitution would work when put to the test. The Louisiana Purchase was a good test.

The story of the Louisiana Purchase is filled with secret deals and bold action. How did President Jefferson go from offering to buy a port to buying such a vast territory? Read on to find out.

## A Sweet Deal

The Louisiana Purchase cost the United States $15 million. That may sound like a lot of money, but it was a great bargain for America. In fact, it has been called the sweetest real estate deal in U.S. history. All that land cost about three cents per acre (about 4/10 of a hectare)!

# Chapter 1

# History of the Louisiana Territory

The Louisiana Territory had been a hot spot for European control as early as the seventeenth century. France controlled the land for most of that time. That changed in the eighteenth century. European countries were fighting the Seven Years' War.

In 1762, Spain got the land west of the Mississippi River. In 1801, France got the land back. Napoléon Bonaparte, emperor of France, made a treaty with Charles IV, king of Spain. Napoléon wanted to make his American colonies stronger. The treaty was called the Treaty of San Ildefonso. America didn't find out about the treaty until later. This is because the talks between France and Spain were kept secret. Also, communication between Europe and America happened by ship. Ships took at least a month to cross the Atlantic Ocean and to bring news.

Meanwhile, Americans had settled in the Louisiana Territory. They depended on being able to trade on the Mississippi River. They also depended on the right of deposit at the port of New Orleans. To have the right of deposit meant that America could deposit, or store, goods in warehouses at the port until those goods were ready to be shipped elsewhere. Whoever controlled the territory could make things hard for American settlers.

Napoléon Bonaparte, pictured here, was the emperor of France during the fight for control over the Louisiana Territory. Napoléon eventually sold the land to the United States at the price of $15 million.

In 1802, Spanish officials in New Orleans said Americans had no right of deposit. President Jefferson was not sure whether Napoléon had told Spanish officials to say this. Americans worried that Napoléon might stop Americans from using the Mississippi River. President Jefferson worried that Napoléon might attack the United States and that he might use the Louisiana Territory as a base. America waited to see what would happen next. President Jefferson told Robert R. Livingston, the American ambassador to France,

This is a picture of Charles Maurice de Talleyrand, Napoléon's adviser. He helped negotiate the selling of the Louisiana Territory. He worked directly with Robert R. Livingston, the American ambassador to France, on the deal.

to talk to Napoléon's adviser, Charles Maurice de Talleyrand. Jefferson told Livingston to find out whether France actually controlled the land. Then Livingston was to try to buy New Orleans from France.

Negotiation with Talleyrand went back and forth for months. Finally, Livingston hinted to Talleyrand that America might just want to stop fighting with Britain. This made the French government nervous. France and Britain were at war. France did not want America to be a British ally. Also, war costs a lot of money. Napoléon decided to sell the Louisiana Territory so that he could pay for the war with Britain.

James Monroe arrived in Paris as President Jefferson's special minister. Neither Livingston nor Monroe had been told to buy the entire Louisiana Territory. Jefferson had sent Monroe with instructions to pay up to $10 million for New Orleans and the Floridas. However, the deal that Napoléon offered was too good to pass up. A treaty was signed on May 2, 1803, but it was dated April 30. The United States paid $15 million. Part of the sum, $11,250,000, was paid right away. The rest of the sum was paid in the form of America erasing debts that France had with America.

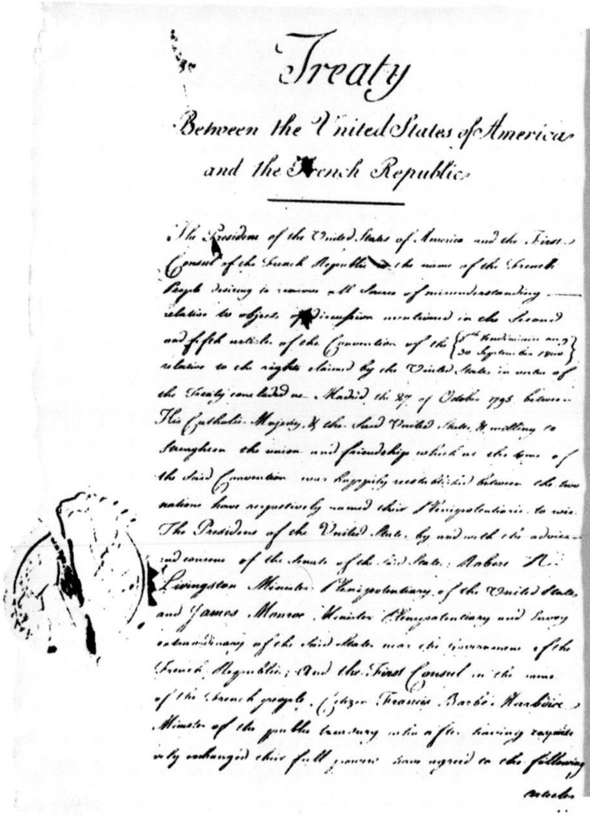
Treaty

Between the United States of America and the French Republic

This is a reproduction of the Louisiana Purchase Treaty. This treaty was an agreement between France and the United States. The treaty states that land that once belonged to France was given to the United States for a sum of money. This meant that the United States was now able to expand.

The words of the treaty were not clear about whether West Florida was part of the territory. Later, America claimed that it was. Spain and France both claimed that West Florida was not part of the Louisiana Purchase. There was one thing that was absolutely clear. The Louisiana Purchase allowed the United States to go ahead with westward expansion.

# Westward Expansion  Chapter 2

The Louisiana Purchase allowed America to settle its western frontier. Many people thought America should be settled from the Atlantic Ocean to the Pacific Ocean. This idea was called Manifest Destiny. Some people had already settled in the western territory. However, before the area was really settled, President Jefferson sent people to explore the area.

In 1804, President Jefferson sent two men, Meriwether Lewis and William Clark, to explore the Louisiana Territory. On May 14, 1804, they began what was called their Voyage of Discovery. Lewis and Clark found out as much as they could about the territory. They led the voyage, but they were not the only ones who went on the trip.

About fifty men and Lewis's dog, Seaman, went with them. They were looking for a water source, such as a river, that would go all the way to the Pacific Ocean. Along the way they found out about many plants and animals. For example, they discovered small animals that looked like squirrels with short tails. They called them prairie dogs because they barked like dogs.

William Clark (*left*) and Meriwether Lewis (*right*) started out on an exploration of the Louisiana Territory in 1804. They explored the Missouri River and wrote down their observations in journals. Their trip was called the Voyage of Discovery.

They also met Native American groups and learned their languages. In October 1804, Lewis and Clark met a Native American woman named Sacagawea. She lived with the Mandan and Hidatsa peoples, along the Missouri River. She had been stolen years ago from her own people, the Shoshone. They lived west, in the Rocky Mountains. She married Touissant Charbonneau and had a son with him, named Jean Baptiste. Sacagawea and Jean Baptiste traveled with Lewis and Clark. She could speak many different native languages. She helped Lewis and Clark talk with the Native Americans whom they met on their voyage.

There were many exciting points in the journey. Lewis and Clark saw the Rocky Mountains. They worked hard to cross the mountains. Sometimes the horses would fall off the steep cliffs.

## The Great Falls

The Mandan, a tribe of Native Americans, told Lewis and Clark that there were waterfalls along the route they were taking. In June 1805, they came across the Great Falls. The Great Falls were made of five waterfalls, not just one. Lewis and Clark and their group had to carry their boats and supplies over land to avoid the falls. They carried all their belongings for eighteen miles (twenty-nine kilometers).

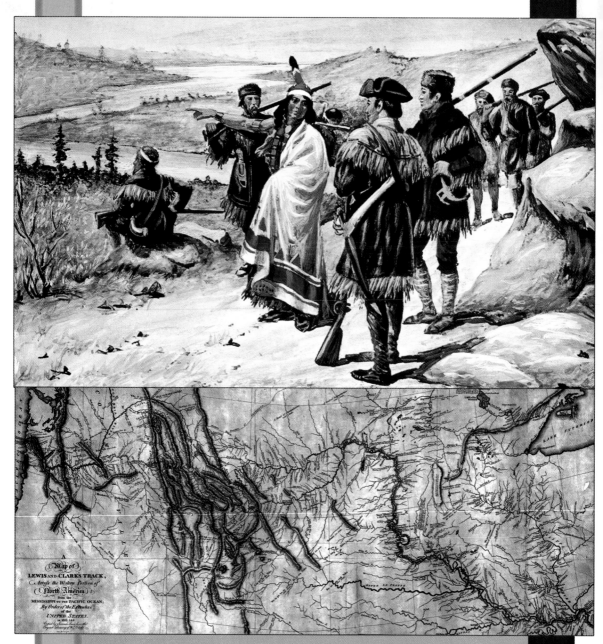

The Lewis and Clark expedition helped the westward expansion of the United States. The explorers saw many new things and met native people on their journey. Sacagawea, a Native American woman, joined Lewis and Clark on their adventure (*top*). The expedition took them across the western portion of the United States (*bottom*).

Lewis and Clark wrote about their trip in journals. They also made maps of the land. They described three hundred different plants and animals. On September 23, 1806, Lewis and Clark finally got back to St. Louis, Missouri, where they had started. Crowds of people greeted them in the street with cheers.

The westward expansion was an exciting chapter in American history. People traveled west along the Oregon Trail in covered wagons. These settlers left everything behind to make a new life in the West. Some people made their livings in the mountains of the West. These men were called mountain men. They hunted animals and sold the skins to make money.

The California gold rush was another major event in the westward expansion. John Marshall worked for John Sutter at Sutter's Mill. Marshall found gold in a stream at Sutter's Mill. People came from all over once they found out that there was gold on the land. Some people even came from as far away as China! They made the long trip to California in hopes of becoming rich from finding gold. Many towns sprang up because of the gold rush.

# Chapter 3    Constitutional Concerns

The U.S. Constitution is the document upon which the U.S. government is based. Many groups in America get their rights because such rights were written into the Constitution. Groups as different as the local church group and the gun club owe much to the Constitution. However, many events went into the shaping of the Constitution. Different events in history raise questions about the Constitution. The Louisiana Purchase was an event that caused many people to consider the Constitution differently.

In 1802, the Constitution was still fairly new. Lawmakers and citizens alike had questions about what the Constitution did and did not allow. The Louisiana Purchase was unlike anything that had

The Constitutional Convention resulted in the creation of the U.S. Constitution (*top*). This painting by Howard Chandler Christie (*bottom*) was created in 1940, more than 150 years after the document was approved.

# Chapter 4

## How the Purchase Shaped America's Future

In the last chapter, we saw how the Louisiana Purchase created unrest about the number of slave states and free states. A slave state was a state in which slavery was allowed. A free state was a state in which slavery was not allowed. The Missouri Compromise was one of the ways in which the government dealt with citizens' concerns about slave states and free states. By 1818, there were enough people in Missouri to make it a state instead of just a territory. Many of its settlers had come from the South.

Congress tried to keep a balance of free states and slave states. Missouri would be a slave state. Maine was made a state around the same time as

This is a railway map of Missouri. Before slavery was ended, Missouri was a slave state. That means people were allowed to own slaves in this state. Slavery was a major political issue in the 1800s. Northern states and southern states disagreed about whether or not it should be allowed. This led to the Civil War, after which slavery was ended once and for all.

Missouri. Maine would be a free state. When those two territories became states together, there would still be a balance of slave states and free states. However, some members of Congress were unhappy about some laws Missouri had about slaves. These members wanted to make an amendment to the Constitution. What finally happened was called the Missouri Compromise.

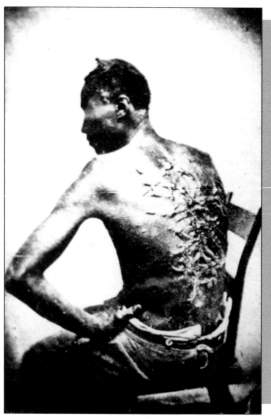

Historically, slaves were treated very poorly. They were often beaten and mistreated. Here, a slave from Louisiana named Peter poses for a picture. He explained, "I was two months in bed sore from the whipping." His scars show how poorly he was treated. It was not unusual for a slave owner to mistreat his or her slaves.

Missouri was made a state, but it had to make changes to its laws in order to become a state.

Before the Louisiana Purchase, most Americans lived in the states and territories between the Atlantic Ocean and the Mississippi River. After the Louisiana Purchase, Lewis and Clark explored and mapped the area. Settlers flocked to the western frontier.

This painting of the explorer Meriwether Lewis was created in 1806. The artist was Charles Julien Fevret de Saint Memin. In part because of Lewis, the United States was able to begin its westward expansion, or grow westward. Lewis and Clark explored the western area of the United States, and people were encouraged to move there.

25

The wave of settlers to the western frontier gave rise to the idea of a transcontinental railroad. There were already many railroads in the East. Theodore Judah was a railroad engineer in the East. He wanted to build a transcontinental railroad. Many people did not agree with Judah's idea. They thought it would be too hard to do. Judah and his wife moved to California in 1854. He built the state's first railroad. Then, in 1861, he met Leland Stanford, Charles Crocker, Mark Hopkins, and Collis Huntington. They were rich businessmen who shared Judah's idea for a transcontinental railroad. They formed a company called the Central Pacific Railroad Company. The main line of their transcontinental railroad was finished in 1869.

Clearly the Louisiana Purchase had much to do with making the United States the country that it is today. It is because of the Louisiana Purchase that Americans were able to settle the western frontier. The western frontier was filled with people who are a special part of American history. Explorers, mountain men, and gold seekers are a colorful part of America's past. The Louisiana Purchase allowed Americans to dream large dreams and to accomplish them. One such accomplishment was creating the transcontinental railroad. Adding the Louisiana Territory made the United States one of the largest nations in the world. As a result, European nations had more respect for the United States

This photograph was taken on May 10, 1869. It shows workers celebrating the completion of the first transcontinental railroad link. The Louisiana Purchase contributed to the expansion of the United States in many ways. The United States not only gained more land, it gained big ideas.

as a nation. In addition, the questions that were raised about the Louisiana Purchase caused many Americans to think hard about the Constitution. It is the raising of such questions that helps to keep America's government one that is run by the people and for the people.

# Glossary

ally (A-ly)  A country that supports another country.

ambassador (am-BA-suh-der)  An official representative of one country who visits another country.

amendment (uh-MEND-ment)  An addition or change to the U.S. Constitution.

compromise (KOM-pruh-myz)  An agreement.

Congress (KON-gres)  The part of the U.S. government that makes laws.

debts (DETS)  Things that are owed.

Democratic-Republicans (deh-muh-KRA-tik rih-PUH-blih-kenz)  People who believed that government power should rest with representatives elected by citizens.

deposit (dih-PAH-zit)  To leave behind.

Federalists (FEH-duh-ruh-lists)  People who supported a union of states under a strong central government.

**frontier (frun-TEER)** The edge of a settled country, where wilderness begins.

**journals (JER-nuhlz)** Notebooks in which people write their thoughts.

**Manifest Destiny (MA-nih-fest DEHS-tih-nee)** The belief that Americans were meant to settle the western part of the United States.

**political parties (puh-LIH-tih-kul PAR-teez)** Groups of people that have similar beliefs in how government affairs should be run.

**Senate (SEH-nit)** A lawmaking part of the U.S. government.

**slavery (SLAY-vuh-ree)** The practice of one person "owning" another person.

**transcontinental (tranz-kon-tin-EN-tul)** Going across a continent.

**warehouse (WER-hows)** Building in which items are stored until they are needed.

**westward expansion (WEST-werd ek-SPAN-shun)** The movement of settlers into the western part of the United States in the 1800s.

# Web Sites

Due to the changing nature of Internet links, the Rosen Publishing Group, Inc., has developed an online list of Web sites related to the subject of this book. This site is updated regularly. Please use this link to access the list:

http://www.rosenlinks.com/lnan/lopu

# Primary Source Image List

Page 1: Louisiana Purchase Treaty from 1803. Housed in the National Archives and Records Administration.

Page 5: Portrait by Thomas Scully. Created in 1821.

Page 6: Panoramic map created in 1885. Created and published by Currier & Ives, New York.

Page 10: Portrait by Pierre Paul Prudhon. Created in 1814.

Page 14 (left): Portrait by Charles Willson Peale. Created in 1810. Housed in the Independence National Historical Park.

Page 14 (right): Portrait by Charles Willson Peale. Created in 1807. Housed in the Independence National Historical Park.

Page 16 (top): Painting by Alfred Russell. Created in 1904.

Page 16 (bottom): Map copied by Samuel Lewis from original drawing by William Clark and Samuel Harrison. Created in 1804.

Page 19 (top): The Constitution of the United States of America was signed on September 17, 1787, establishing the government of the United States. Housed in the National Archives and Records Administration.

Page 19 (bottom): Painting by Howard Chandler Christie. Created in 1940. Housed in the United States Capitol Historical Society.

Page 23: Map completed in January 1888. Created by R. T. Higgins.

Page 24: Photo taken on April 2, 1863. Housed in the National Archives and Records Administration.

Page 25: Portrait by Charles Julien Fevret de Saint Memin. Created in 1806.

Page 27: Photo taken by Andrew Russell on May 10, 1869.

# Index

## About the Author

Magdalena Alagna is a freelance writer and editor living in New York City.